Score with Sports Math

Score with Soccer Math

Stuart A. P. Murray

Enslow PUBLISHING

Published in 2013 by
Enslow Publishing
2544 Clinton Street
Buffalo NY 14224

Library of Congress Cataloging-in-Publication Data

Murray, Stuart, 1948-
Score with soccer math / Stuart A.P. Murray.
pages cm. — (Score with sports math)
Includes index.
Summary: "Get fun soccer facts while practicing math techniques such as addition, subtraction, and geometry. Also includes math problem-solving tips"—Provided by publisher.
ISBN 978-0-7660-4175-2
1. Soccer—Mathematics—Juvenile literature. I. Title.
GV943.25.M88 2012
796.334—dc23

2012028799

Future editions:
Paperback ISBN: 978-1-4644-0289-0
EPUB ISBN: 978-1-4645-1181-3
Single-User PDF ISBN: 978-1-4646-1181-0
Multi-User PDF ISBN: 978-0-7660-5810-1

Printed in the United States of America
10 9 8 7 6 5 4 3 2 1

To Our Readers: We have done our best to make sure all Internet Addresses in this book were active and appropriate when we went to press. However, the author and the publisher have no control over and assume no liability for the material available on those Internet sites or on other Web sites they may link to. Any comments or suggestions can be sent by e-mail to comments@enslow.com or to the address on the back cover.

Design and Production: Rachel D. Turetsky, Lily Book Productions

Illustration Credits: © Amy Taylor-Murray, p. 17; © 2012 Clipart.com, pp. 4, 5, 12, 23, 37; Doug James/Photos.com, p. 41; fstockfoto/Shutterstock.com, p. 6; © iStockphoto.com/Talaj, p. 25; Kirk Strickland/Photos.com, p. 28; Laszlo Szirtesi/Shutterstock.com, p. 5; luoman/Photos.com, p. 13; Maxisport/ Shutterstock, pp. 34, 35, 38; Mikkel William Nielsen/Photos.com, p. 45; Natursports/Shutterstock.com, pp. 18, 30 (top); Rafael Ramirez Lee/Shutterstock.com, p. 8 (inset); Shutterstock.com, pp. 2, 6, 15, 16, 32, 33 (top), 37, 42, 43; Wikimedia/Ampatent, p. 19; Wikimedia/Boston Public Library, Print Department, p. 14; Wikimedia/Dagur Brynjólfsson, p. 33 (bottom); Wikimedia/Dipanker Dutta, p. 8; Wikimedia/dontworry, p. 42; Wikimedia/Jarrett Campbell, p. 24; Wikimedia/Joel Solomon, pp. 22 (left), 46; Wikimedia/John Mena, pp. 7, 22; Wikimedia/Matthew Beckler, p. 40; Wikimedia/Nationalencyklopedin, p. 26; Wikimedia/Simo82, pp. 30 (bottom), 31, 35; Wikimedia/Ysangkok, p. 10.

Cover Photo: Anne-Louise Quarfoth/Photos.com

Contents

Introduction: Soccer: The World's Game 4

1 On the Playing Field 9

2 Goal Scoring: Strikers and Midfielders 19

3 Defending: Keepers, Sweepers, and Stoppers 29

4 Last Chance to Win 39

Math Problem-Solving Tips 46

Further Reading: Books and Web Sites 47

Index 48

The goalie saves a penalty kick in the European Champions League final.

INTRODUCTION

Soccer:

The World's Game

Soccer is the world's most popular team sport. Most people in the world call it "football." It got this name because it was played on foot instead of on horseback.

Early football was wild and rough and played by hundreds on each side. Players moved a ball across a field and could kick, punch, or carry it.

When the Pilgrims landed in America in 1620, they found that the local Wampanoag people played the same sport. The Pilgrims and Wampanoags soon were playing football on the beach with a deerskin ball. By the 1800s, Americans came to call it "soccer."

In this book you'll learn some soccer facts and history, and you'll practice math, too. Knowing math makes playing or watching soccer even more exciting.

Scoring goals and winning leagues

Nowadays, soccer is played by kicking and heading the ball. Only goalies may catch, throw, or punch the soccer ball.

Wherever soccer is played, scoring is the same: Put the ball in the other team's goal. There are plenty of soccer statistics (stats), and the most important is goals. But for a team to win the league, it's points that count: a team gets 3 points for each win and 1 for each tie.

Strikers try to lead the league with the most goals scored. Goalies want to have the lowest goals allowed average. There's more than just a league championship to play for, though.

There are competitions between teams from every country. And there are worldwide tournaments for men's and women's teams.

The greatest tournament is the World Cup, which is played every four years. The winning country can claim their national soccer team is the best in the world.

Spain won the 2010 World Cup.

World Cup USA '94 and '99

Mia Hamm, left, is the all-time U.S. women's team scoring leader with 158 goals.

There are two World Cups: one for women and one for men. The first men's World Cup played in the United States was in 1994. More than 3.5 million fans came to the games, breaking the record by more than 1 million. Millions more watched on television in every country. World Cup USA '94 was one of the greatest in history.

In 1999, the Women's World Cup was held in the United States for the first time. The American women's soccer team has been one of the world's best. In 1999 it won the Women's World Cup for the second time.

The American soccer tournaments were so successful that in 2003 the Women's World Cup was again held in the United States.

1

On the Playing Field

Around the world more than 250 million people play soccer. Their fields should be at least 100 yards long and 50 yards wide. But soccer fields come in many different sizes, depending on where they are located.

Crowded neighborhoods in many countries have only a small space for goals and a playing area. In the United States, high school campuses often have several full-size fields. And some European stadium fields are huge: 120 yards long and 75 yards wide!

Whatever the field's size, the object is to go for the goal!

Young men play muddy soccer in Kolkata, India.
(Inset) Bernabéu stadium in Madrid, Spain.

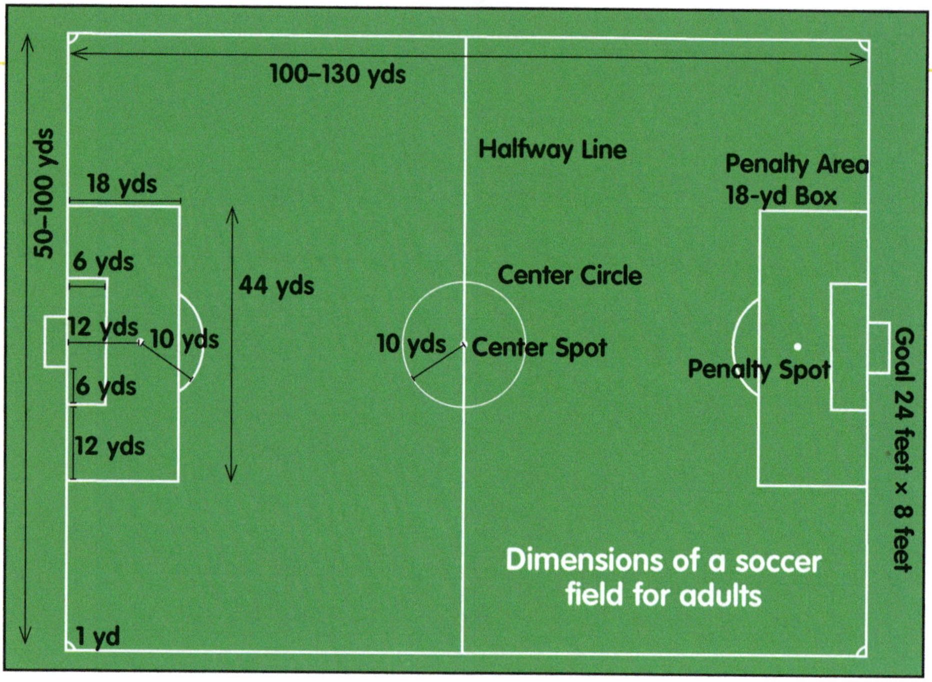

Soccer fields and stadiums

The length and width of a soccer field for adults can vary, but the measurements around the goal area stay the same. The penalty box is 18 yards wide and 44 yards long.

Q: What is the perimeter of the penalty box?

A: The perimeter is the distance around the penalty box. This is found by adding the widths and the lengths of all four sides.

44 + 18 + 44 + 18 = 124 yds

Major League Soccer (MLS) is the leading professional soccer league in the United States and

Canada. The MLS has 19 teams. The 10 largest stadiums are listed in the chart below.

Q: Which stadium has the largest playing field?

A: Real Salt Lake: 130 yds long by 90 yds wide

Q: How much older than the newest stadium is the oldest stadium?

A: Oldest: Portland, 1926; newest: Houston, 2012
Subtract the oldest from the newest.
2012 – 1926 = 86 years

The 10 largest MLS stadiums

Team	City	Year Built	Capacity	Field Size
Seattle Sounders	Seattle, Wash.	2002	38,500	114 by 74 yds
Los Angeles Galaxy	Carson, Calif.	2003	27,000	120 by 75 yds
New York Red Bulls	Harrison, N.J.	2010	25,000	120 by 75 yds
Houston Dynamo	Houston, Tex.	2012	22,000	115 by 70 yds
Toronto	Toronto, Ont.	2007	21,859	115 by 74 yds
Vancouver Whitecaps	Vancouver, B.C.	1983	21,000	117 by 75 yds
Dallas	Frisco, Tex.	2005	20,500	117 by 74 yds
Portland Timbers	Portland, Oreg.	1926	20,438	110 by 70 yds
Montreal Impact	Montreal, Que.	2008	20,341	120 by 77 yds
Real Salt Lake	Sandy, Utah	2008	20,213	130 by 90 yds

Pro soccer's fastest-growing league

The MLS was established in 1993. In 2011 it had 19 teams. Total attendance at all the games in 2011 was 5,460,000. There was an average of 17,872 fans per game.

Q: If every team drew exactly the same number of fans in 2011, what would be the average attendance per team?

A: Divide 5,460,000 by 19.

5,460,000 ÷ 19 = 287,368 fans

In 2011, the Seattle Sounders led MLS in average game attendance: 38,496. The San Jose Earthquakes had the lowest: 11,858.

Q: How much higher average attendance than San Jose did Seattle have?

A: Subtract San Jose's average game attendance from Seattle's average.

38,496 – 11,858 = 26,638 more fans

Maracanã, in Rio de Janeiro, Brazil, was redesigned with seating to hold 82,238 fans.

Brazil: A world leader in attendance

Maracanã Stadium in Brazil opened in 1950 for the World Cup. The final game had 199,854 fans. Most people stood. The highest attendance for a U.S. match between club teams was 93,137 at the Rose Bowl in Los Angeles, in 2009, when Spain's Barcelona defeated the L.A. Galaxy 2–1.

Q: Estimate to the nearest thousand how much bigger the Brazil crowd was than the L.A. crowd.

A: Round off attendance totals to the nearest thousand: 200,000 and 93,000.

Subtract 93,000 from 200,000:

200,000 – 93,000 = 107,000

The Brazil crowd had about 107,000 more fans.

Winslow Homer illustrated the start of an 1857 soccer match at Harvard; the Rutgers–Princeton game might have looked like this.

Football, soccer, and bans

In 1869, Rutgers and Princeton played a "football" game: no hands allowed. American football historians say it was the first college football game. But it was soccer. The score: Rutgers 6, Princeton 4.

Q: As an "American football" game, with 6 points for a score, what would the score be?

A: Multiply each team's score by 6:
Rutgers: 6 × 6 = 36
Princeton: 4 × 6 = 24

Assoc + er = soccer

In 1880, soccer was called "association football." This was shortened, and "assoc" became "soccer." Only the United States, Canada, Australia, New Zealand, and Ireland call it soccer.

Q: There are 209 national soccer associations in the world. Five use the term "soccer."

A: What percent calls the game soccer?
Divide 209 into 5:
5 ÷ 209 = .02, or 2 percent

Banning women's soccer

The first official women's soccer match was in London in 1895. Soon, crowds of 50,000 watched women's games. But in 1921 British football officials banned women from club fields. This ban was not lifted until 1969.

Q: For how many years was women's soccer banned from British clubs?

A: Subtract 1921 from 1969:
1969 – 1921 = 48 years

Soccer for everyone

There are many different types of soccer: outdoor, indoor, college, high school, youth, beach, soccer on water, five-a-side, wheelchair, soccer for the deaf, freestyle juggling, and of course street soccer.

Soccer is played around the world in sandlots, on streets, and wherever else there is a place to play.

Q: A regular soccer ball is 8.6 inches in diameter. A wheelchair soccer ball is 4.4 inches larger. What is the diameter of a wheelchair ball?

A: Add 8.6 inches and 4.4 inches.

8.6 + 4.4 = 13 inches in diameter

The United States has the most youth soccer players in the world.

More than 5 million players are on organized youth soccer teams in the United States. Millions more play in local recreation leagues.

Q: A youth soccer tournament has 8 fields in use. Each field has 2 teams with 8 players per team, and 1 ref. How many people are on all the fields?

A: Multiply 8 fields by the 2 teams on each field:

8 x 2 = 16 teams in total

Then multiply 16 teams by 8 players per team:

16 x 8 = 128 players

8 games with 1 ref each means 8 referees. Add players and referees:

128 + 8 = 136 people

adidas
bwin

2

Goal Scoring: Strikers and Midfielders

The crowd cheers for the perfect goal. A midfielder makes a great pass to the striker, who hits the ball perfectly. The goalie has no chance.

But when a team needs to score, the crowd roars just as loudly for the "garbage goal." That's when the ball goes in after bouncing around close to the goal. No perfect strike, but players who have good scoring instincts—a "nose for goal"—put these away.

And at the final whistle, the garbage goal counts just the same as the perfect goal.

Real Madrid's Cristiano Ronaldo is one of the world's top scorers.

Ball possession and scoring

The team with the most goals wins a game. Teams that keep the ball the longest (possession) have more time to score. Spain's Barcelona is one of the best ball-possession teams. They once had the ball for 73 percent of a game.

Q: The game lasted 90 minutes. How long did Barcelona have the ball?

A: To find 73 percent of 90 minutes multiply 90 by .73.

90 × .73 = 65.7 minutes

Abby Wambach of the U.S. Women's National Team (WNT) scores so often that possession is less important when she plays. As of 2011, she'd scored 191 pro goals. Including her goals scored in college, she has a total of 287.

Abby Wambach was the leading career goal scorer among U.S. women playing in 2012.

Q: How many college goals did Wambach score?

A: She scored 191 pro goals. Subtract 191 from her total of 287:

287 – 191 = 96 goals in college

Q: In college she had 10 "hat tricks," or 3 goals in a game. How many goals did she have in those 10 games?

A: Multiply 10 by 3:

10 × 3 = 30 goals

Wambach pro stats

Team	Games	Goals
WUSA	86	53
WNT	182	138
Total	268	191

Q: How many more goals did she score for the Women's National Team (WNT) than in the Women's United Soccer Assoc. (WUSA)?

A: Subtract her WUSA goals from her WNT goals:

138 – 53 = 85 goals

Q: Find how many more pro games she played than goals she scored.

A: Subtract total goals, 191, from total games, 268:

268 – 191 = 77 more games

Kristine Lilly (above) of the United States played in five Women's World Cups. Megan Rapinoe (left) starred on the U.S. team that won the 2012 Olympic gold medal.

Women's soccer and World Cup

American women's soccer is one of the world's best. The first Women's World Cup was held in China. The United States won. Each World Cup tournament starts with 16 teams in 4 groups, A–D.

Q: The first Women's World Cup was played in 1991, 61 years after the first men's World Cup. What year was the first men's World Cup?

A: Subtract 61 from 1991.

1991 – 61 = 1930

The top two teams in each group advance. If their points are the same, then the one with the better "goal differential" (GD) ranks higher. GD compares goals for (GF) with goals against (GA).

Team	Tournament Points	W	D	L	GF	GA	GD
United States	6	3	0	0	11	2	?
Sweden	4	2	0	1	12	3	?
Brazil	2	1	0	2	1	7	?
Japan	0	0	0	3	0	12	?

The chart shows the results of Group B in the 1991 Women's World Cup. Teams earned 2 points for a win and 1 for a draw.

Q: Figure out each team's goal differential (GD).

A: Subtract the goals against (GA) from goals for (GF). The team with the higher GD is above any team that has the same number of points (P).

USA: 11 – 2 = 9

Sweden: 12 – 3 = 9

Brazil: 1 – 7 = –6

Japan: 0 – 12 = –12

Landon Donovan, left, is not only a top scorer, but is also a tough midfielder.

Goals and assists

One or two of the eleven players on a team are strikers. Four or five are midfielders, who play defense and also help by giving assists. An "assist" is a pass to the scorer. Some midfielders, such as Landon Donovan, are scorers and also assist leaders.

MLS all-time top scorers (regular season)

Goals leaders		Assists leaders	
Player	Goals	Player	Assists
Jeff Cunningham	134	Steve Ralston	135
Jaime Moreno	133	Carlos Valderrama	114
Landon Donovan	119	Preki	112
Ante Razov	114	Jaime Moreno	102
Jason Kreis	108	Marco Etcheverry	101
Taylor Twellman	101	Landon Donovan	97
Dwayne De Rosario	98	Cobi Jones	91

Q: Which players are top scorers and also leaders in assists?

A: Jaime Moreno (133 goals and 102 assists) and Landon Donovan (119 goals and 97 assists).

In its first years, MLS figured scoring leaders by giving 2 points for a goal and 1 for an assist. The "Golden Boot" award went to the player with the most points.

Q: Who would have the most points, Donovan or Moreno?

A: Multiply each player's goals by 2. Then add his assists.

Moreno: $133 \times 2 = 266$

$266 + 102 = 368$

Donovan: $119 \times 2 = 238$

$238 + 97 = 335$

368 (Moreno) – 335 (Donovan) = 33

Moreno would have 33 points more.

Pelé leads Brazil against a Swedish club in 1960.

The greatest scorers in history

The chart below includes all goals scored by top scorers in their professional and amateur careers. Four of these top five scorers averaged more than a goal a game.

Total career goals

Player	Country	Years	Games	Goals
Josef Bican	Aust. & Czech.	1931–1956	918	1,468
Gerd Müller	Germany	1962–1983	1,216	1,461
A. Friedenreich	Brazil	1909–1935	1,239	1,329
Pelé	Brazil	1956–1977	1,366	1,282
Franz Binder	Aust. & Ger.	1930–1949	756	1,006

Q: Which player had the longest career?

A: Subtract each player's first year from his last. Do the subtraction for all 5 sets of years.

1956 – 1931 = 25 years (Bican)

1983 – 1962 = 21 years (Müller)

1935 – 1909 = 26 years (Friedenreich)

1977 – 1956 = 21 years (Pelé)

1949 – 1930 = 19 years (Binder)

Now find the largest number: Friedenreich had the longest career with 26 years.

Brazil's Pelé was the most famous soccer player of the twentieth century. He helped Brazil win three World Cups.

Q: How many more goals did Pelé need for an average of 1 goal a game? To have an average of 1 goal per game, the number of games needs to equal the number of goals.

A: Pelé scored 1,282 goals in 1,366 games.

Subtract 1,282 from 1,366:

1,366 – 1,282 = 84 more goals

11
16

3

Defending: Keepers, Sweepers, and Stoppers

The offense usually gets the credit when a team wins. But the offense can't do anything if the defense doesn't do its job.

That defense's job is to stop the other team's attack and win the ball back. A goalie makes the save or a defender tackles the ball away, and then the team goes on offense. Every attack starts with a good pass from the back.

For a striker to have chances to score, he needs to have a good defense behind him.

A goalie makes a save during a youth tournament game.

Defenders have to be good headers to keep the ball from the attackers.

Defensive shapes

Soccer positions are organized into various formations, or shapes. Sometimes there's a single last defender, called a "sweeper." This player's job is to "sweep up" balls that get past the main line of defenders. The diagrams show defenders (blue), midfielders (yellow), and attackers (red).

The "sweeper formation" has a final defender.

Q: How many midfield players are there in the formation on the opposite page?

A: Four: the yellow circles.

Q: How would you describe this formation in numbers? Don't count the goalie.

A: From back to front: 1-3-4-2.

Modern soccer teams put as many players as possible on defense. This makes it more difficult for the opponent to score. In the formation at right, the two central midfielders are also defensive players.

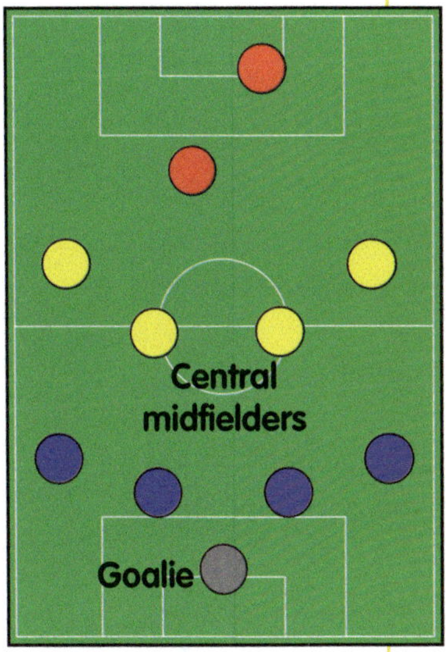

In this formation, the two central midfielders play more defensively.

Q: Count the number of players on defense.

A: There are 7 on defense: 4 backs (blue), 2 central midfielders (yellow), and 1 goalie (gray).

Q: How would you describe this formation in numbers? Don't count the goalie.

A: From back to front: 4-4-1-1.

Goalies dive through the air to make saves.

Goalie: The toughest position

Goalkeeping is the most difficult position in soccer. A keeper has to dive, block shots, and jump. Good keepers make great saves. But when goals go in, it's a terrible feeling.

Q: The goal is 24 feet wide and 8 feet high. A yard is 3 feet. What is the width of the goal in yards? The height in yards?

A: For the width in yards, divide 24 feet by 3.
$24 \div 3 = 8$ yds wide
For the height in yards, divide 8 feet by 3.
$8 \div 3 = 2\frac{2}{3}$ yds high.

Q: A tall goalkeeper standing in the middle of the goal spreads his arms 8 ft wide. What fraction of the width of the goal is the goalie's arm spread?

A: The goalie's arm spread divided by the total goal width is $8/24$. Reduce the fraction by dividing both the numerator and denominator by 8. $8/24 = 1/3$. The goalie's arm spread covers $1/3$ of the goal.

In 2012, American keeper Brad Friedel set the English Premier League record of 310 starts in a row. The previous record holder was English goalie David James with 166 consecutive starts.

Friedel stars in the English Premier League.

Q: How many more consecutive starts did Friedel have than James?

A: Subtract 166 from 310:

310 – 166 = 144 more starts

Q: Friedel has played a total of 639 pro club games and 82 games for the U.S. men's national team. What is the total of these games?

A: Add 639 and 82:

639 + 82 = 721 games

Liverpool's Steven Gerrard is a midfielder who is excellent on both defense and attack.

Defensive midfielders and center backs

Defensive midfielders play in front of the defensive backs and attack when their team gets the ball. They run more than most players. They might cover 7 miles a game, often sprinting.

Q: The midfielder runs 5.6 miles in a game, sprinting half the time. How far does he sprint?

A: Divide 5.6 by 2:

$5.6 \div 2 = 2.8$ miles sprinting

The center back stops attacks up the middle. Modern soccer has two center backs (stoppers) who play between the two fullbacks.

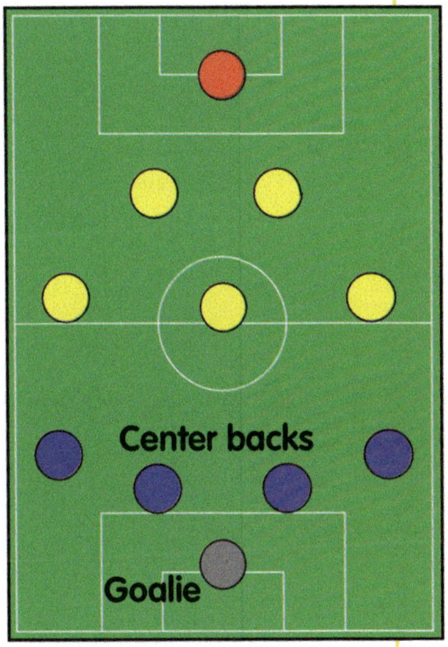

The 4-3-2-1 formation has two center backs in the middle.

Q: What fraction of the total defenders (blue circles) are center backs?

A: 2 divided by 4 is $\frac{2}{4}$. Reduce the fraction: $\frac{2}{4} = \frac{1}{2}$

$\frac{1}{2}$ of the defenders are center backs.

Q: A center back touches the ball 56 times in a game. One fourth of those touches are head balls. How many headers did the stopper make?

A: Divide 56 by 4.

$56 \div 4 = 14$ headers

Defenders in an Italian league game form a wall to block a free kick's direct line to the goal.

Set plays and penalties

Defenders have to prevent opponents from scoring during "set plays." These are free kicks and corner kicks. An attacker sends the ball close to the goal for teammates to get, or shoots right at the goal.

Q: Defenders form a wall 10 yards from the kicker and 25 yards from the goal. How far is the kicker from the goal?

A: Add 10 yds and 25 yds:

10 yds + 25 yds = 35 yds from kicker to goal

Only the goalie can stop a penalty kick. The ball is placed just 12 yards from the goal. The keeper doesn't have much chance.

Q: A penalty kick travels about 60 yds per second. About how long does it take to reach the goal?

A: The ball is placed 12 yds from goal, so divide 12 by 60: $^{12}/_{60}$.

Reduce the fraction by dividing both the numerator and denominator by 12.

$^{12}/_{60} = {}^{1}/_{5}$

The ball reaches the goal in $^{1}/_{5}$ of a second.

Studies show that pro goalies save 15 percent of penalty shots that are on the goal.

Q: A goalie faces 100 penalties and all are on the goal. How many will he probably save?

A: Write 15 percent as a fraction: $^{15}/_{100}$

Multiply 100 by $^{15}/_{100}$.

$100 \times {}^{15}/_{100} = 15$ penalties saved

33

4

Last Chance to Win

United and the Eagles are in a championship play-off. United loses the first game at home, 0–2. Now they must play at the Eagles' home stadium. The team with the most total goals from both games wins the championship.

Can United get at least two more goals than the Eagles? They'll have to score early to keep the Eagles from playing tight defense.

The team that scores first has a big advantage. So, United has to come out strong. They want to get that first goal to help them win the championship!

It takes teamwork to score goals and win games.

The final game

To reach the two-game championship play-off, the teams first played in a "knockout" tournament of 16 teams. This means teams were knocked out of the first rounds as soon as they lost one game.

Q: How many rounds were needed before the championship play-off?

A: 3 rounds.

16 teams played in 8 games for the first round.

8 teams were left for the second round.

4 teams were left for the third round.

2 teams are left for the final championship play-off.

For teams to meet in the finals, each has to start in a different group of eight teams.

In the first game United had 45 percent of ball possession.

Q: What percent possession did the Eagles have?

A: Subtract 45 percent from 100 percent:

100 – 45 = 55 percent possession for the Eagles

Keeping the ball is key to a good offense.

At the kickoff, the United striker surprises the Eagles by passing the ball 10 yards forward to his teammate who takes a long-range shot. The goalie is too far out, and the ball flies in! United 1–Eagles 0.

Q: The field is 110 yards long. The kickoff from the center spot is at the halfway line. How far did the shot travel?

A: From the halfway line to the goal is ½ of 110:

110 ÷ 2 = 55 yds

Subtract 10 yds for the forward pass:

55 – 10 = 45 yds

The keeper palms away a fierce shot.

A shot-stopping goalie

It's said that a good goalkeeper will make a good team great. The United goalie is very good and stops every shot from the Eagles. The first half ends United 1–Eagles 0.

Q: What is the score combining goals from both games?

A: The Eagles scored 2 goals in the first game. United scored only in this game so far: 1 goal. The play-off score is Eagles 2–United 1.

In the second half a United player is fouled. United scores with a free kick to take a 2–0 lead. The total score for both games is now 2–2.

The match is 90 minutes. There will be 3 minutes of "extra time" added for breaks during the game. The Eagles get a penalty kick in the 83rd minute!

Q: How much time is left?

A: Subtract 83 from 90:

90 – 83 = 7 minutes

Add the extra time:

7 + 3 = 10 minutes left

Most goalies guess and dive to one side or the other. By diving, the goalie's body covers $\frac{1}{9}$ of the total area of the goal. If the goalie stays standing, arms spread, then $\frac{1}{3}$ of the goal area is covered.

Q: Which method covers more of the goal: diving or standing?

A: $\frac{1}{9}$ means the goal is divided into 9 parts and 1 part is covered; $\frac{1}{3}$ means the goal is divided into 3 parts and 1 part is covered.

$\frac{1}{3}$ is more than $\frac{1}{9}$, so standing covers more goal.

The United goalie remains standing and blocks the penalty! The play-off stays tied.

A penalty shooter begins her run at the ball.

Penalty shootout

The game goes into overtime: two 15-minute periods. After an exciting overtime, the play-off score is still tied, United 2–Eagles 2.

Q: How many total minutes were played by the end of overtime?

A: Multiply 15 by 2 and add the original 90 minutes.

15 × 2 = 30 minutes

30 + 90 = 120 minutes total

Now the championship will be decided by a penalty shootout. Five players from each team will take turns shooting.

A study of 300 pro penalty shots showed that 171 were aimed at the lower third of the goal. About 80 percent scored.

Q: About how many goals were scored by shooting low? (Round the answer.)

A: Find 80 percent of 171 by multiplying 171 by .8.

$171 \times .8 = 137$ goals

This penalty study showed that only 13 percent were aimed at the upper third of the goal. But all of them scored!

Q: How many goals were scored by shooting higher?

A: Write 13 percent as a fraction: $^{13}/_{100}$

Multiply 300 by $^{13}/_{100}$

$^{13}/_{100} \times 300 = 39$ goals

The United players all knew about this study. All five aimed at the upper third of the goal. They won the shootout 5–4, and the championship!

The shooter shows good form in his approach.

Math Problem-Solving Tips

- Always read the problem completely before beginning to work on it.
- Make sure you understand the question.
- Some problems take more than one step to find the final answer.
- Don't think you always have to use every number in the problem. Some numbers are extra information that are not needed for the calculations.
- If you know your answer is wrong but can't find the mistake, then start again on a clean sheet of paper.
- Don't get upset! You can solve problems better when you're calm.
- If you're stuck on a problem, skip it and go on with the rest of them. You can come back to it.

The U.S. Women's National Team celebrates their gold medal victory over Japan in the 2012 Olympics.

Further Reading

Books

American Education Publishing (compiler). *The Complete Book of Math, Grades 3 and 4.* Greensboro, N.C.: American Education Publishing, 2009.

Connolly, Sean. *The Book of Perfectly Perilous Math.* New York: Workman Publishing Company, 2012.

Fitzgerald, Theresa. *Math Dictionary for Kids.* Waco, Tex.: Prufrock Press, Inc., 2011.

Web Sites

Drexel University. The Math Forum @ Drexel University. 1994-2012.
<http://www.mathforum.org/k12/mathtips>
K–12 math problems, puzzles, and tips and tricks. The Math Forum of Drexel University is a leading online resource for improving math learning, teaching, and communication.

Ellen, Stephanie. Soccer Related Math Projects.
<http://www.ehow.com/list_6382698_soccer-related-math-projects.html>
A variety of soccer-related projects you can make for your math class. "From algebra to geometry, there's math in every aspect of the game."

Index

A
addition, 16–17, 20, 25, 27, 36, 44
American football, 14
assists, 24–25
Association Football, 14–15
average, 5, 12, 21, 26–27

B
ball possession, 20, 41

C
center back, 34, 35
center circle, 10, 41
common divisor, 10
corner kick, 36

D
diameter, 16
dimensions, 10
division, 10, 12–13, 15

E
estimate, 13, 41

F
football, 4–5, 14–15
formations, 30–31, 35
free kick, 36, 42

G
"garbage goal," 19
goal, 29, 31–33, 36–37, 43, 45
goal area, 10
goal differential, 23
goalkeeper, 4–5, 19, 28–33, 37, 41–45
goals, 5, 7, 9–10, 19–27, 31, 39, 41
goals against, 23
goals per game, 21
Golden Boot Award (MLS), 25

H
hat trick, 21
heading, 5, 30, 34–35

M
Major League Soccer, 11–13, 24–25
midfielder, 19, 24–25, 30–31, 34–35
multiplication, 14, 17, 20–21, 25, 37, 44–45

N
national associations, 15
national teams, 6–7, 20–21, 33

O
Olympic Games, 22

P
penalty kick, 4, 36–45
penalty box, 10, 44
penalty shootout, 44–45
percent, 15, 20–21, 37, 41, 45
playing fields, 4, 8–15, 17, 41
play-off, 39–45

R
radius, 10, 41
rounding, 13, 21, 37

S
saves, 4, 29, 32, 37
shooting, 36, 41, 44–45
soccer football, 5
soccer, types of, 16
spectators, 12–13
stadiums, 8–13, 39
stopper, 29, 35
striker, 5, 19, 24, 29, 41
subtraction, 11–12, 15, 22–23, 27, 33, 35, 37, 41, 43
sweeper, 29–31

T
tournaments, 6, 7, 17, 22, 29, 40

W
wall (defensive), 36
wheelchair soccer, 16
Women's United Soccer Association, 21
World Cup, Men's, 6–7, 13, 22
World Cup, Women's, 7, 22–23

Y
youth soccer, 16–17, 29